JENNY ROSSITER

NOBLER AND BETTER THINGS

OCTAVIA HILL'S LIFE AND WORK

First published in 2012

Octavia
Emily House
202-208 Kensal Road
London, W10 5BN

T   020 8354 5500
E   info@octavia.org.uk
W   www.octavia.org.uk

ISBN 978-0-9573073-0-8

 Design & layout by Avenue Design
www.avenuelondon.co.uk

OCTAVIA HILL

CENTENARY 1838–1912

OCTAVIA HILL BLUE PLAQUE, RED CROSS GARDENS

London Borough of Southwark

Octavia Hill

Social Reformer

Established this garden,
hall and cottages,
and pioneered
Army Cadets
1887-90

Voted by the People

CONTENTS

INTRODUCTION

A nti-social behaviour, binge drinking, debt, poverty and a lack of good affordable housing are headaches for today's policy makers, but the Victorian social reformer Octavia Hill was grappling with the same issues nearly 150 years ago. She set about tackling these problems with tenacity and vision, befriending working people and marginalised communities, whilst mobilising the middle classes to provide both money and volunteers. Her ideas and solutions grew out of her personal contact with families living in the city's slums; and in her own lifetime she had a lasting impact on the living conditions of the urban poor.

Octavia Hill's most enduring legacy was the method of housing management she devised to provide healthy, affordable dwellings for low income tenants living in appallingly squalid and overcrowded conditions. But her reforming influence was felt in many areas of Victorian life. As part of her housing work she developed new approaches to social work and charitable giving. She believed that art and beauty should enhance the lives of all people and not be a preserve of the wealthy. She organised cultural events in deprived areas. The term green belt was first coined by Octavia Hill. She pioneered the open space movement and was one of the founders of the National Trust to provide amenities *"for ever for everyone"*.

We can be grateful to Octavia Hill for the relatively clean air we breathe in our cities today. Her campaign for smoke abatement in the 1880s laid the foundations for clean air legislation in the twentieth century. Her interest in the welfare and development of young people led her to set up an Army Cadet Corps in a working class area of London. Above all, she was concerned with the totality of an individual's life – his or her physical, social, cultural, economic and natural environment.

RED CROSS COTTAGES AND GARDENS
WAS DEVELOPED IN 1886

Some of her views on social policy and housing are at odds with mainstream thinking today. Nevertheless, in the late nineteenth century Octavia Hill anticipated many of the questions that we are grappling with today, including welfare dependency, community cohesion and the relationship between the voluntary sector and the state.

STEPS IN
OCTAVIA HILL'S LIFE

FAMILY, CHILDHOOD
AND EARLY YEARS

Octavia Hill was born in Wisbech, Cambridgeshire in 1838, the eighth daughter (hence her name 'Octavia' from the Latin octo for eight) of James Hill, a well-to-do banker and corn merchant. She was the product of an unusual family. Her maternal grandfather, Dr Thomas Southwood Smith, was an associate of Edwin Chadwick, the pioneer of public health reforms in the early 1800s. Southwood Smith spent much of his time in Spitalfields and Bethnal Green in east London, researching and providing free medical services for the poor. It is believed that the hero of Charles Dickens' *Bleak House*, a doctor working in a slum district, is based on him, and he certainly provided the novelist with first hand accounts of child labour, city slums and conditions in the Cornish tin mines.

Her father, James Hill, was a follower of Robert Owen, the industrialist and advocate of practical socialism, who spent his life trying to improve the working conditions, homes and education of ordinary people. Hill was a campaigning reformer, who started a local newspaper, *The Star in the East*, which sympathetically covered news of the radical Chartist and Owenite movements. When he met Caroline Southwood Smith, he was a widower with five daughters and one son. Caroline was employed as the family governess and they married in 1835. Together they had five more daughters, including Octavia.

Caroline was a teacher and writer and was said to be the first Englishwoman to use the methods of the Swiss educational reformer, Johann Pestalozzi. She and her husband set up an infant school in

Wisbech in 1837 and ran it according to Pestalozzi's ideas – abandoning teaching by rote and formal religious education, and encouraging children to develop at their own pace. In her writings on education she advocated Pestalozzi's approach, stressing her antipathy to conventional Victorian ideas of school discipline. Caroline also enchanted her young daughters with the fairy tale *Skyrack*, which she wrote about a North London oak tree believed to have been based on the tree associated with the infamous highwayman Dick Turpin.

In 1840, when Octavia was only two years old, her father declared himself bankrupt. The family was forced to leave Hill's elegant house in Wisbech, and lived in various places, including Gloucestershire and Leeds. During this period, Hill suffered a mental breakdown and the family broke up, with Caroline taking her own five daughters (Miranda, Gertrude, Octavia, Emily and Florence) and eventually settling in East Finchley, then a rural outpost of London. Caroline was greatly helped by her father who gave her financial support and provided a home for Gertrude.

Octavia's childhood was far from affluent, but her mother gave her a love of the arts and literature and an awareness of injustice in the world. Even as a child Octavia showed her determination to act on her beliefs. She did not take sugar, since it was the product of the slave trade and she was moved to write a poem about the Irish potato famine.

ADOLESCENCE AND FORMATIVE YEARS

In 1852 Caroline was appointed manager of the newly founded Ladies' Guild. This was a Christian Socialist cooperative enterprise, teaching craft-making skills to unskilled women and girls. The objects produced, such as dolls and glassware, were then sold. At the age of fourteen, Octavia was given the job of managing the toymakers, a group of poor girls from a Ragged School. The Ragged Schools were charitable schools dedicated to the free education of destitute children. The movement started in Scotland in 1841, initially for boys only but in 1843 they were opened to girls. In 1844, the movement spread to England, with the establishment of the London Ragged School Union under the chairmanship of Anthony Ashley Cooper, 7th Earl of Shaftesbury.

It was from visiting the homes of the Ragged School girls that she obtained her first experience of poverty and housing conditions in London. This venture also brought her into contact with the leaders of the Christian Socialist Movement, including F.D. Maurice, who become her mentor and an influence on her spiritual life. Along with her sisters Miranda and Emily, she was baptised and confirmed in the Church of England, leaving the Unitarian church tradition she had been born into. Miranda said that Octavia's faith was the *"underlying motive and guide for the whole of her life"*.

In 1853 John Ruskin, the great art critic and social reformer, visited the Ladies Guild and met the fifteen year old Octavia for the first time. This was the beginning of a long, and at times turbulent, relationship. Octavia later trained as a copy artist under the guidance of Ruskin, and was able to use her artistic skills to earn a steady income. She was employed by Ruskin as a copyist for one volume of his major work *Modern Painters*. Although their relationship fractured in 1877, Octavia was strongly influenced by his ideas. Their differences stemmed from the fact that Octavia based her actions on practical experience and observation, while Ruskin was far more utopian and idealistic in outlook - many of his practical projects failed.

In 1855 F D. Maurice began courses for women at the Working Men's College in London, and the following year he invited Octavia to become part-time secretary to the women's classes. In this role she assumed responsibility for financial transactions and bookkeeping, which would help her in her future housing management work. She combined this with teaching arithmetic and brought in additional money by giving tutorials in bookkeeping.

In 1862 Octavia and her sisters established a small school in Nottingham Place, Marylebone. She taught drawing and practical bookkeeping and continued a connection with the school until its closure in 1891. On Saturday evenings every child had to submit the account of their week's pocket money to Octavia and it had to be absolutely accurate.

On his father's death in 1865, Ruskin inherited a considerable sum of money and sought Octavia's advice on how he should use it. She suggested buying and improving homes for poor families. Following her advice, Ruskin bought three cottages of six rooms each in Paradise Place, just round the corner from her own home and school, and placed these houses, which were *"in a dreadful state of dirt and neglect"*, under her management. The following year he acquired the freehold of five other houses for Octavia to manage in nearby Freshwater Place. Thus, at the age of twenty-seven, she began over forty years of housing management in which she sought to improve the homes of many of London's poorest families.

Throughout the rest of her career, Octavia continued to enlarge, through private donations, the portfolio of property she managed. Her management approach was described in her book *Homes for the London Poor*, which was published in 1875. The following year, one of her influential benefactors, Princess Alice, Queen Victoria's second daughter, arranged to get *Homes for the London Poor* translated and distributed in Germany.

Octavia's wider interest in alleviating poverty and in reforming indiscriminate charitable giving developed from her involvement in property. She was invited to join the newly formed Charitable Organisation Society in 1869, and in 1870 assumed the management of some homes in Walmer Street, London, where she inaugurated an *"industrial experiment"*. The idea behind this project was to train and find work for the unemployed men and women among the two hundred or so poor families within the community.

Octavia's only documented romance occurred in 1877 when she was briefly engaged to Edward Bond, a wealthy barrister and a favourite of the philanthropic set. But his widowed mother expressed her displeasure at the partnership and Octavia broke off the engagement. Also, in the same year she was publicly attacked by her patron John Ruskin. Her failed romance, the pressure of her incessant work schedule, the quarrel with Ruskin and the death of two close friends culminated in a severe nervous breakdown. She spent most of the following three years travelling around Europe with Harriot Yorke, who remained her companion for the rest of her life.

THE LATER YEARS

On her return in 1880, Octavia launched herself back into public life with the Kyrle Society, which she had set up in 1877 with her sister Miranda. The Kyrle Society, the forerunner of today's civic societies, had a wide remit, for *"bringing beauty to the people"*, including planting trees, smoke abatement, open spaces provision and promoting art and cultural activities.

In 1884, following her return to housing management work, Octavia gave evidence to the Royal Commission on Housing. She was approached not only by private landlords but by the Ecclesiastical Commissioners to manage and improve their run-down rented properties. In 1886 she was granted a 999-year lease by the Ecclesiastical Commissioners on a plot of land in Southwark. Thus began the development of her much-loved Red Cross Cottages - six small, self-contained cottages, a communal garden and a community hall, reminiscent in style of rural village life, which was restored with a grant from the Heritage Lottery Fund in 2006.

From 1890 onwards much of Octavia's energy was spent on promoting open spaces in London and conserving the natural beauty of the countryside. In 1895 she co-founded the National Trust with Canon

Hardwicke Rawnsley and Robert Hunter, both long term associates and early conservationists.

Her status as a national figure was confirmed in 1887, when she was one of three women invitees, in their own right, to attend Queen Victoria's Golden Jubilee service in Westminster Abbey. The others were Florence Nightingale, the nursing reformer and Josephine Butler, who fought against the abuses of the white slave trade and prostitution. For her sixtieth birthday John Singer Sargent painted a memorable portrait of her, which now hangs in the National Portrait Gallery.

One of Octavia's final challenges was to serve as a member on the Royal Commission on the Poor Law in 1905. She pursued a gruelling travel schedule, visiting and taking evidence in many deprived parts of the country. As always, she had her own strong views on tackling poverty and deprivation without creating dependency on charity or the state. She signed the majority report, but entered reservations on two points: the extension of free health care and the creation of artificial work in periods of recession.

On 13 August 1912 Octavia Hill died peacefully in London and was buried near Larksfield, her final home, in Crockham Hill, Kent, which lies on the edge of a lovely, wooded ridge overlooking the Weald. Her grave is beneath a yew tree in the nearby churchyard, fittingly overlooking Mariner's Hill, one of her earliest acquisitions for the National Trust. Two days after her funeral there was a well-attended memorial service at Southwark Cathedral – only a brief walk from Red Cross Cottages and Gardens.

OCTAVIA HILL'S OCTAGON

Octavia's mark on the world can be summarised under eight headings – an octagon of activities: Housing; Clean Air; Open Spaces; Arts and Culture; Social Work; Employment; Volunteering; and Youth Work. In most of these areas, she left her mark by founding institutions, changing legislation and pioneering procedures and administrative systems. The following pages describe her activities in these eight areas.

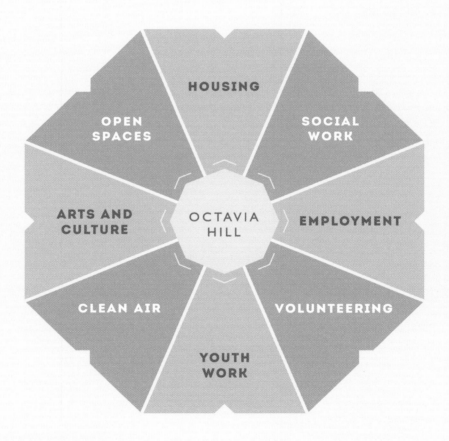

HOUSING

O ctavia was a pioneer of social housing and the founder of the housing management profession, but she believed in providing far more than bricks and mortar. She treated every tenant as an individual and was concerned about all aspects of their welfare, including the quality of air they breathed, their recreational activities and their employment prospects.

The mechanisms she used for providing affordable, healthy accommodation varied according to the source of funding available to her. From 1865 she mobilised financial support and voluntary help mainly from middle-class philanthropists and social reformers and seized opportunities offered by existing landlords to provide and manage better homes for London's poor. There were common features to all her schemes, but she provided homes in three ways.

THE ETHICAL INVESTMENT APPROACH

Long before the term ethical investment was in vogue, Octavia devised a scheme whereby people could use their capital to invest in social housing and still receive a return of five percent a year. It started when Ruskin bought a fifty six year lease on three run-down houses in Paradise Place (now Garbutt Place) in Marylebone, London, in 1865 for Octavia to manage. Ruskin's aim was *"to do justice among the people .... to free a few poor people from the tyranny and influence of a low class of landlord"*. The following year he purchased five additional properties in Freshwater Place and one in Marylebone Road (now Old Marylebone Road) to add to her portfolio.

In subsequent years, other social contacts - and sometimes strangers

- who were impressed by Octavia's methods, purchased property for her to manage. They also received their five percent return. Accounts were kept for every property and she provided each owner with periodic statements of income and expenditure.

When a new property came into her hands, she made sure that it was put into a good state of repair. She attempted to reduce overcrowding and evicted defaulting tenants and those she regarded as *"immoral"*. She insisted on *"extreme punctuality and diligence"* in the weekly payment of rent. Rental income was used to pay rates and insurance and generate the five percent return for owners. Any surplus was used for repairs and improvements as suggested by tenants, including the construction of playgrounds and gardens.

In her *Letter to My Fellow-Workers (LFW)* of 1874 Octavia described how she organised the management of fifteen blocks which contained 2,000-3,000 tenants in total:

> " " *Each block is placed by me under a separate volunteer worker, who has the duty of collecting, superintending cleaning, keeping accounts, advising as to repairs and improvements, and choice of tenants.*

OCTAVIA'S HOUSING MANAGEMENT METHOD

Octavia explained her system of reporting to the members of the Royal Commission on the Housing of the Working Classes in 1884:

Question: In fact you manage the whole affair and furnish them [proprietors] a return at certain times of the year? -

> " " *Half yearly; but as I said the owners are very various, some of them come continually into the courts and see and watch how the thing is going on, and they say to the tenants, would you like this or that done; and sometimes they even collect the rent themselves. Some of them are non-resident, and leave it entirely to me and my friends; it varies very much.*

RANSTON STREET WAS REBUILT
UNDER OCTAVIA HILL'S SUPERVISION

Question: Have you no regular returns and accounts? -

66 99 *There is a separate cash book and ledger for each block of buildings or group of houses ...and those are audited every half-year, and a copy of the accounts with the vouchers sent to the owner; but each one goes to the owner privately.*

Question: So that the returns differ in each case probably? -

66 99 *Yes, they may differ.*

Most properties yielded a four to five percent return, but like all investments they sometimes did not perform as expected. In 1907 Miss Schuster, a key investor, acquired two houses in Notting Hill and placed them under Octavia's management. She subsequently received *"mournful"* reports and accounts revealing cash deficits and an absence of interest payments due to a failure to let all the rooms.

HOUSING TRUST APPROACH

Some of Octavia's supporters simply gave her property. This clearly gave her a good deal of freedom in the use of surplus funds which would have otherwise gone to the owners. Octavia used a Trust structure to manage this part of her housing activities, thereby creating, alongside the Peabody Trust, one of the first not-for-profit housing trusts in Britain. In one of her letters to fellow workers she commented on how this structure generated a continuing flow of income for the trust. All surplus funds were channelled back into projects connected with the organisation.

The Horace Street Trust, was initially set up in 1886 to manage a modest gift of just three properties in Horace Street (now Cato Street) in Marylebone. The Trust steadily accumulated more buildings in a variety of ways – some were given outright, others left as legacies and a few acquired from the surplus cash generated by the organisation. The gifts usually came from friends and acquaintances. The Horace Street dwellings, for example, came from Mrs Anna Scrase-Dickins, one of her principal benefactors, and the Westbourne buildings in Paddington (which now no longer exist) were left to Octavia in 1896 by Emilia Gurney, a member of the original committee of Girton College, Cambridge, and wife of Mr Russell Gurney, a Member of Parliament who campaigned for women's rights. The Trustees, of which the majority were women, were also friends, family and fellow workers – the number was eventually raised from three to five including Octavia and her niece Elinor Lewes.

The deeds of the Trust illustrate the way in which the business was run. They stated that after all necessary housing expenses, including repairs and improvements, had been charged, the surplus could be used for *"open spaces and objects which were helpful to the people" (LFW 1910)*. Great attention was paid to keeping the properties in a good state of repair. In 1903 no profits were taken for the Trust's properties in Ranston Street as it was necessary to put in damp proof courses to render *"the parlours dryer" (LFW 1903)*.

The Trust was also able to raise money from benefactors for specific projects. In 1910 it generated sufficient funds to buy three leasehold properties in Notting Hill *"to prevent them from falling into bad hands"*. Octavia had previously managed these properties for the landlord and was determined that her work with the tenants was *"not broken off"*. Over the years, property was added to the Trust and it continued to function after Octavia's death. In 1921, her favourite project, the Red and White Cross cottages in Southwark, were transferred to it.

Today, after various mergers, Horace Street Trust forms part of Octavia Housing, a housing association which manages over 4000 properties in some of the most expensive areas to live in London.

ADVISOR AND MANAGING
AGENT APPROACH

As Octavia's reputation spread, landlords and property agents approached her to manage their tenanted property, the largest being the Ecclesiastical Commissioners (now the Church Commissioners). In 1884 she took on the management of forty eight properties in Queens Street, Deptford, for a private landlord, who had purchased them thinking he would be richly compensated when a proposed tram-line was built. The tram-line never arrived and the properties became dilapidated and run down. Unlike her other property, these houses presented continuous management problems. Octavia put this down to the fact that the tenants never saw themselves as long-term residents of the area and so were reluctant to get involved with improvement programmes. She referred to this area as the *"black sheep"* of her work.

In the 1880s the Ecclesiastical Commissioners had gained an unwelcome reputation as slum landlords and were eager to employ Octavia to change their public image. She agreed to take on the management of some of their properties in Southwark and Deptford and was later asked to advise on layout and management of new housing schemes. Whenever possible, she tried to persuade the Commissioners to improve existing cottages and houses rather than demolish and replace them with tenement blocks. She believed families were healthier and happier if they had access to their own yard and front door, thus becoming an early advocate of personal defensible space, now a familiar concept. She regarded common stairwells as a particular management problem, as no one took responsibility for cleaning and policing them.

If shortage of land or economics meant that tenement blocks were the only option, Octavia advised that there should be plenty of open space and light. She believed that only two dwellings on each floor should share a common stair-well, and she cautioned that blocks should be no higher than four stories. Today, in Short Street and Mitre Road near Waterloo Station, blocks that were built in 1903 with advice from Octavia are still occupied by tenants.

In Walworth in south London, she was delighted that, on her advice, the Commissioners replaced their slum housing with 790 dwellings – four-roomed and three-roomed cottages, cottage flats, and flats in tenement blocks no higher than three storeys high. These Arts and Craft style homes were completed in 1906 and for a hundred years formed part of the Octavia Hill Estate in South London. This long history of management came to a controversial end in February 2006, when the Church Commissioners sold the entire estate of 1,130 homes to a partnership that included a property developer and a housing association. Some of the homes will remain as affordable rented housing and some will be sold off to private owners.

In 1886 the Commissioners granted Octavia a 999-year lease on a plot of land in Southwark where slum clearance had taken place. It was on this plot that she developed her much cherished project of Red Cross Cottages, garden and hall.

RED CROSS GARDEN

The six four-roomed cottages in Red Cross Street, completed in 1888, together with the adjacent hall and garden, represented Octavia Hill's vision of affordable rented housing in a community setting. She described the hall, as the *"parish parlour"*. It was used as a library and reading room and at times was the venue for theatre, music and dance performances. In White Cross Street, abutting the rear of Red Cross Street, six more cottages were built and completed in 1889. All the cottages, designed by Elijah Hoole, are in a rural village style. The garden was laid out with flower beds and offered an open space in which residents could relax. Today all the houses are occupied by tenants of Octavia Housing. The garden has been renovated by the Bankside Open Spaces Trust and was reopened in June 2006 by The Princess Royal.

In all the property Octavia managed, either as an agent, owner or tustee, she was diligent about eradicating over-crowding, carrying out repairs and improvements and establishing firm but friendly face-to-face contact with tenants. By the end of her life she had created the profession of housing management and trained many women in the skills of community management. Through her methods of personal contact and support for tenants, she had shown that it was possible to rent houses to disadvantaged, poor families and still make a surplus. Her aim was to make *"lives noble, homes happy and family life good"*. She firmly believed that, given the right housing conditions, physical environment and access to opportunities, working people could better themselves.

In relation to the size of London's housing problem at the time, her work was not on a large scale. Nevertheless, she improved the life of thousands living in London's slums and she established a distinct model of housing management. In her own lifetime her methods attracted considerable interest and were adopted in one form or another by other British cities and several countries overseas, including Holland, South Africa and the USA.

Although she was against public subsidy for housing, she was only able to achieve her goals by using three identifiable forms of informal or community subsidy. Firstly, she had access to cheap investment capital from her contacts and friends, which enabled her to buy property to rent and improve. Secondly, she relied on an army of mostly middle-class, socially-minded women to manage the housing. Nearly all were volunteers. She trained them, but their services were free. And thirdly, in the case of the Red Cross Cottages, she was provided with the land at a nominal ground rent from the Ecclesiastical Commissioners.

She used these informal subsidies to find creative and ingenious solutions to the housing problems of her time. She had enormous tenacity and was prepared to be flexible to get things done. Later on in

WHITE CROSS COTTAGES - DEVELOPED IN 1890

her life she saw the advantages of involving local authorities in social housing, but she believed that they should be enablers rather than providers. She made this point clear in 1899, when she supported the wish of the newly constituted London County Council for abundant and cheap housing, while insisting that the Council should not run the accommodation itself.

OPEN SPACES

The hundreds of walkers, joggers, kite flyers, lovers, children and dogs that enjoy the grassy slopes of Parliament Hill every day owe an enormous debt to Octavia. Parliament Hill is one of the highest points in North London and has commanding views over the city. In the latter half of the nineteenth century property developers were moving remorselessly into this part of London, reducing the open spaces available to the city's rapidly growing population. By this time Octavia had become a fierce advocate of open spaces for city dwellers. She saw the opportunity to pursue this ambition by securing Parliament Hill, and other pieces of land, for public use.

In 1875 she wrote an essay *Space for the People* in which she outlined her thoughts on why people needed certain types of open spaces. From her observations of the crowded housing tenements, she believed that conditions could be ameliorated by the *"healing gift of space"*. At times she thought it more beneficial, especially in the summer, to provide open space for people than to improve their housing conditions.

〈〈 〉〉 *In the summer the people drink more, live more in public, and there is more vice. Sometimes on such a hot summer evening in such a court when I am trying to calm an excited woman shouting their execrable language at one another, I have looked up and seen one of those gleams of light that summer sun sends out just before he sets... But to me it brings sad thoughts of quiet places far away where it is falling softly on tree and hill and I feel as if that quiet, that space could be more powerful to calm the wild excess about me than all my frantic striving with it.*

Her views on access to open space were more collective and radical than her approach to housing:

66 99 *the house is an individual possession and should be worked for, but the park or the common which man shares with his neighbours, which descends as a common inheritance, surely this may be given...*

She identified the need for four types of open space: places to sit in; places to play in; places to stroll in; and places to spend a day in.

In the crowded and fetid parts of the city, people needed places near their homes that were clean and airy to sit in. She thought disused churchyards should be opened to the public for recreational purposes, and successfully persuaded the authorities to refurbish and open the gates to many of London's graveyards and churchyards – these included Drury Lane churchyard, St Anne's Soho, St John's Waterloo, and St Peter's Bethnal Green. Today, these spaces are still enjoyed by residents and city workers for relaxation or a quiet out-door lunch.

Octavia always had her eye open for small parcels of land that could be saved from the developers and cultivated as parks. One of these was Hilly Fields in Lewisham, South London, that she first heard of when visiting one of her tenants in Deptford. Seeing a bunch of wild flowers in one of the houses she enquired where they came from and was told about this piece of open ground. In a letter to the Daily Graphic in 1892 she described her new discovery:

66 99 *I went to seek out the spot, and found it absolutely bounded on the London side by ... little houses, but commanding, on the south, a view far away to Knockholts Beeches.*

Today this park still offers South Londoners wonderful views over the Kent countryside beyond the intervening suburbs.

When Octavia started her housing work she was conscious that children needed supervised playgrounds to play in, apart from the streets and alleys. Ruskin enabled her to create her first open space behind the houses in Freshwater Place. He owned the freehold of these properties and was able to demolish the dilapidated out-houses and construct a garden and play area. Through donations, swings and railings were provided and a supervisor, probably a retired tenant, was employed to keep an eye on things.

Octavia thought the London Embankment and Royal Parks were great places in which people could stroll and relax. But she was concerned that many of the families living in the poorer areas of London did not use these open spaces. She wanted them to realise that these areas were not the preserve of the wealthy and could be used by anyone. Thus on summer evenings she organised walks in the parks for people with *"no gardens, backyards or second rooms"*.

She had thoughts of *"places to stroll in"* when she started her campaign to secure, in perpetuity, Parliament Hill, North London, for public use. She wrote;

66 99 *these fields have been our constant resort for years: they are within easy reach for most of us, and a two penny train takes the less vigorous within a few yards of the little white gate by which they are entered. They are the nearest fields on our side of London and there on a summer Sunday or Saturday evening you might see hundreds of working people, who have walked up there from the populous and very poor neighbourhoods of Lisson Grove and Portland Town.*

Besides securing public access to land spaces on the outskirts of London through the National Trust, she also provided *"open spaces to spend a day in"* by organising day excursions to the countryside for groups of up to 200 tenants. Octavia was a formidable networker, and she managed to persuade many of her wealthy friends to open their houses and gardens for the use of her tenants from London's tenements. By 1874 she was organising up to fifteen excursions during the summer months and on more than one occasion she hired a river steamer for the event. Her half brother, Arthur, often entertained dozens of tenants at his house just outside Reading, and her nephew, the Rev. Fredrick Hill, also allowed his vicarage at Shere in Surrey to be used for summer parties. In the Jubilee year of 1897 she organised a trip for another group to Southend.

Much of her campaigning for open spaces was done through the Kyrle Society which raised funds for numerous open space projects, of which the largest were Vauxhall Park, Parliament Hill and Hilly Fields in Lewisham.

Many of the small open spaces she secured for public use are still used. But today they are frequented by city workers seeking peace and quiet from the stress of the office and traffic congestion rather than by slum dwellers escaping overcrowded and fetid tenement blocks. Many of these London open spaces are listed at the end of the book.

Her open space campaigning brought her into contact with Robert Hunter, a lawyer to the Commons Preservation Society (today known as the Open Space Society), who later became one of the founding members of the National Trust, along with Canon Hardwicke Rawnsley and Octavia herself. As a young man Rawnsley collected rents for her in Drury Lane and by the 1880s he was fighting to preserve tracts of land in the Lake District from the developers. Seeing the need for an organisation that could combine campaigning with the power to acquire land, they established the National Trust in 1895.

Initially the National Trust was concerned with the preservation of the countryside from developers but later it started to purchase historic and notable property for the nation. Some of the earliest National Trust land acquired was near Octavia's home in Kent. This included Mariner's Hill, Toys Hill and Ide Hill, all close to her grave in Crockham Hill Church.

UFFORD STREET - REDEVELOPED IN 1903

WESTMINSTER

1. 14 Nottingham Place, where Octavia lived between 1860 & 1891.
2. 190 Marylebone Road (now Marathon House), where Octavia lived until her death in 1912.
3. 207 Old Marylebone Road, community centre for Freshwater Place.
4. 25 Paddington Street, Ruskin's tea shop managed by Octavia.
5. 31 Upper Montague Street, home of Grandfather Dr Thomas Southwood Smith.
6. Barrett's Court (now St Christopher's Place) 1869 Octavia starts management of these properties.
7. Bell Street, first buildings constructed for Octavia by Elijah Hoole.
8. Bryanston Square, St Mary's. Octavia worked in this parish with Rev Samuel Barnett.
9. Charles Street (now Ranston Street) rebuilt under Octavia's supervision.
10. Cosway Street, Christ Church where Octavia was confirmed.
11. Francis Street Westminster, where Octavia lived in 1859.
12. Freshwater Place, purchased by John Ruskin in 1866 for Octavia to manage.
13. Horace Street (now Cato Street) formed part of Horace Street Trust in 1886.
14. Lisson Grove.
15. Manchester Square/ Manchester Street, home to the Kyrle Society.
16. Marylebone Road (now Old Marylebone Road) where in 1869 Octavia begins to manage eleven properties purchased by Lady Ducie and Mrs Stopford Brooke.
17. Milton Street (now Balcombe Street) where Octavia Lived in 1859.
18. Ossington Buildings.
19. Paradise Place, (now Garbutt Place) purchased by John Ruskin in 1865 for Octavia to manage.
20. Walmer St and Walmer Place purchased in 1870, site of the Walmer Street Industrial Experiment.

CAMDEN

1. Highgate cemetery, where Octavia's mother and sister Florence are buried.
2. Red Lion Square, Working Men's College where Octavia worked as a secretary in 1856.
3. Russell Place Bloomsbury where she lived in 1852.
4. Queen's Square, Working Women's College, where Octavia taught in 1864.

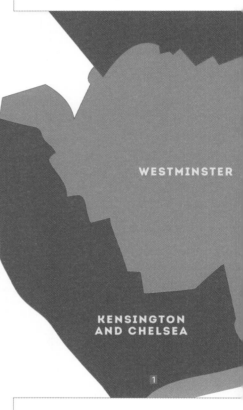

WESTMINSTER

KENSINGTON AND CHELSEA

KENSINGTON AND CHELSEA

1. Church Street, Hereford Buildings.

OCTAVIA HILL'S LONDON

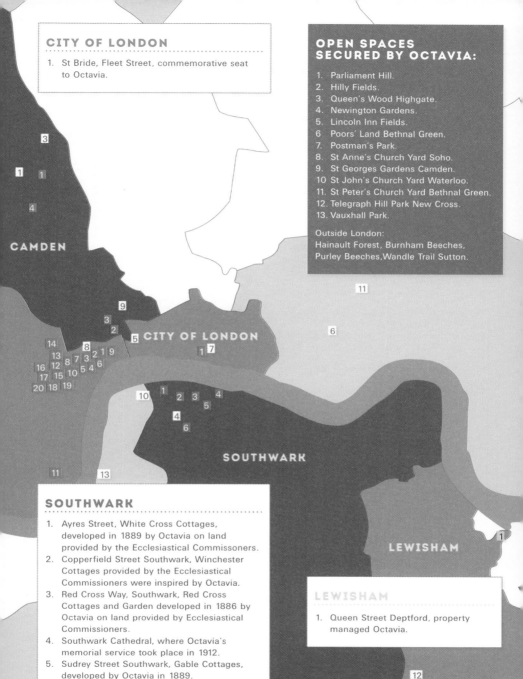

CITY OF LONDON

1. St Bride, Fleet Street, commemorative seat to Octavia.

OPEN SPACES SECURED BY OCTAVIA:

1. Parliament Hill.
2. Hilly Fields.
3. Queen's Wood Highgate.
4. Newington Gardens.
5. Lincoln Inn Fields.
6. Poors' Land Bethnal Green.
7. Postman's Park.
8. St Anne's Church Yard Soho.
9. St Georges Gardens Camden.
10. St John's Church Yard Waterloo.
11. St Peter's Church Yard Bethnal Green.
12. Telegraph Hill Park New Cross.
13. Vauxhall Park.

Outside London:
Hainault Forest, Burnham Beeches, Purley Beeches, Wandle Trail Sutton.

CAMDEN

CITY OF LONDON

SOUTHWARK

LEWISHAM

SOUTHWARK

1. Ayres Street, White Cross Cottages, developed in 1889 by Octavia on land provided by the Ecclesiastical Commissioners.
2. Copperfield Street Southwark, Winchester Cottages provided by the Ecclesiastical Commissioners were inspired by Octavia.
3. Red Cross Way, Southwark, Red Cross Cottages and Garden developed in 1886 by Octavia on land provided by Ecclesiastical Commissioners.
4. Southwark Cathedral, where Octavia's memorial service took place in 1912.
5. Sudrey Street Southwark, Gable Cottages, developed by Octavia in 1889.
6. Walworth Estate, properties owned by Ecclesiastical Commissioners, redeveloped with advice from Octavia in 1903.

LEWISHAM

1. Queen Street Deptford, property managed Octavia.

POSTMAN'S PARK WAS OPENED IN 1898

ART AND CULTURE - BRINGING BEAUTY TO THE PEOPLE

A s a child, many of Octavia's formative years were spent in what were then the semi-rural villages of Finchley and Highgate in North London. This was still an area of open fields, trees and streams running down to the Thames, a leafy playground for the Hill children which Octavia would recall nostalgically in later life. Her mother even wrote a children's story inspired by a local oak tree.

The experience of growing up in this environment left Octavia with an inextinguishable love of the countryside and a firm belief that nature can exercise a beneficial influence on behaviour. She combined this feeling with the notion that artistic expression and the appreciation of art and poetry could also enhance people's lives. Once again, her personal experience had led her to this conclusion – as a copy painter with Ruskin she had learned about art and design, and her understanding of art was deepened by contact with several celebrated Victorian artists including Walter Crane, Holman Hunt, G F Watts and William Morris. She was also fond of the Victorian tradition of reading poetry aloud: she was said to read Browning, one of her favourite poets, *"beautifully"*.

Octavia was keen to promote the love of art and beautiful things among the working classes. Partly with this in mind she founded the Kyrle Society[1] with her sister Miranda in 1877. While the Kyrle Society was best known for providing open spaces, it was equally concerned

---

[1]   The Kyrle Society was named after John Kyrle (1637-1724) of Ross on Wye who served the poor, built alms houses and improved the facilities of his town. He is commemorated in lines by Alexander Pope in his Epistle to Bathurst.

with promoting the decorative arts, music and literature. Octavia said its aim *"was to mitigate the dreariness of towns"* by diffusing *"a love of beautiful things among our poor brethren"*.

The Society pursued its objective of bringing *"beauty home to the poor"* by a variety of means: it decorated public spaces such as hospital wards, parish rooms and mission halls with murals, mosaics and paintings, it distributed books and magazines and it organised musical performances. A remarkable number of its supporters were well-known designers, artists and architects, including William Morris and Lewis F Day. Many were involved in the emerging Arts and Crafts movement. Despite Octavia's work with Ruskin, a passionate supporter of the avant-garde, semi-impressionist paintings of J M W Turner, her own preferences in art, design and literature were for the Pre-Raphaelites, the nostalgic Arts and Crafts style and the romantic poets.

This rather traditional view of art and culture was propagated by Octavia in the activities she organised for working people at the Red Cross Hall in Southwark. These included flower shows, musical recitals - including renditions of Handle's Messiah – drama productions and art and craft classes. After one performance of the Messiah, Octavia wrote *"the Hall was crowded to overflowing and it was wonderful to watch the faces of rough men and toil-worn women listening with rapt attention to the music and carefully following the words"*.

The houses, garden and hall of the Red Cross development were intended as a model of a city community which could be replicated across London – an unattainable target given the rapid increase of London's population and the pressure on land. Nevertheless, her vision of city life coincided with the views of the thinkers and planners who promoted the Garden City movement and later the New Town developments fifty or sixty years later. Sadly, the only feature in the garden to survive today is *The Sower*, a mosaic roundel made by James Powell, a leading glass and tile maker of the time.

The Red Cross Hall was in need of internal adornment when it was opened in 1888 and it was decided to commission a work of art depicting popular heroism. Walter Crane, a popular artist, was appointed to paint wall murals for the hall and money was raised through an appeal in *The Times*. The design for the scheme comprised a series of panels illustrating acts of working class heroism, including a local heroine Alice Ayres, who lost her life while trying to rescue two children from a burning house. None of these panels has survived to the present time, but a commemorative tile to Alice Ayres is displayed in Postman's Park – one of the open spaces in the City of London secured by Octavia.

As well as in the Red Cross Hall, Octavia also encouraged cultural and recreational activities in St Christopher's Hall at Barrett's Court (now St Christopher's Place behind Oxford Street). Here from the late 1880s there were regular annual productions of Gilbert and Sullivan operettas – the cast made up of workers and tenants.

THIS PLAQUE WAS GIVEN BY
M^{iss} JULIA MINET
AND ERECTED BY M^{iss} OCTAVIA HILL
IN 1896
IT WAS RESTORED IN 1956 BY
THE HORACE STREET TRUST

THE SOWER MOSAIC ROUNDEL BY JAMES POWELL
IS THE ONLY ORIGINAL FEATURE IN RED CROSS
GARDENS TO SURVIVE

SOCIAL WORK

In addition to her pioneering work in housing management, Octavia is regarded by some as a major inspiration in the development of modern social work. In particular, she established the concept of the casework approach in her own work, a method that was adopted and emulated by others.

At the outset of her involvement in housing, her main goal was to help people help themselves and become independent of charity. She individualised each case and situation and believed in the value and dignity of even the most bedraggled of her tenants. She insisted that all her housing managers treated everyone with respect and that a caring relationship was the basis of the work. All these values are central to what later became known as social work.

An institutional milestone in the development of the profession was the formation of the Charity Organisation Society (COS), which was founded in 1869 by Octavia and Edward Denison, a prominent philanthropist known for his work in east London. The COS was opposed to indiscriminate alms giving and believed that charity should be dispensed in such a manner as to enable the recipient to become self-supporting. State intervention, it believed, should be kept to a minimum.

The greatest contribution of the COS was to pioneer the system of investigation into the conditions of the recipients through its volunteer and, later, paid workers. This was a continuation of Octavia's approach of devising solutions that were dependent on a comprehensive knowledge of the "whole circumstances" of each family. Material relief on the basis of assessed needs of the person was to be given, but just as important was the influence of the COS visitor in changing the life pattern of the family.

In Victorian Britain, there were innumerable charities to assist the poor and destitute. The Times reported in 1885 that the combined income of the London-based charities alone came to more than the revenue of several European governments. Octavia and others were concerned about the uncoordinated and overlapping activities and the nature of the work of these burgeoning philanthropic organisations. Initially named the Society for Organising Charitable relief and Repressing Mendicity, the COS worked to coordinate the fundraising and the disbursement of funds in a systematic fashion. The intention was to have a COS district committee covering each of London's poor law districts so there could be liaison between charities and poor law guardians.

At its most influential, the COS had 40 local committees functioning across London. Octavia never wavered from its general principles but others, including Cardinal Manning, Beatrice Webb and the Barnetts[2], later questioned and veered away from the idea of placing total emphasis on the individual. They were more inclined to the view that poverty could be tackled both on an individual and collective basis.

During its existence the organisation was responsible for England's first labour exchange, setting up tuberculosis dispensaries, meal centres and thrift clubs. Later it founded the Institute of Hospital Almoners and started the School Care Service to deal with social problems affecting school children. In 1938 it opened the first Citizens Advice Bureau. Over the years, it has altered its emphasis and today its work continues through the Family Welfare Association, which has pioneered change in the health and social services sectors.

A tenant's view of Octavia's social work approach was reported back to her by Canon Barnett:

> 66 99 It is charity and it is not charity – it's charity because it is human kindness: it's not charity because it does not make people cringe".

---

2   Cardinal Manning was a convert to the Roman Catholic Church and became its leader in England and Wales in 1875. He was responsible for the building of Westminster Cathedral and was involved in many social issues including settling the London Dock Strike in 1889. Beatrice and her husband Sidney Webb were socialist activists, leaders of the Fabian Society and the Labour Party, and founders of the London School of Economics. Samuel Augustus Barnett was a clergyman and social reformer and together with his wife Henrietta (nee Rowland) they established the first University settlement at Toynbee Hall in East London in 1884.

CLEAN AIR

ondon began to be known as *"the big smoke"* in the 1700s and its thick *"pea-souper"* fogs first appeared in the 1840s – phenomena that were immortalised in JMW Turner's painting of *London from Greenwich Park*, in which the fog lies heavily over the scene. It may be that Octavia's interest in clean air was first sparked by this painting – in her early years she copied paintings for Ruskin, who was a prominent advocate of Turner.

There were Smoke Nuisance Acts in 1858 and 1866, and further regulation in the Public Act of 1875. But these measures neither touched on domestic smoke nor provided for an official air monitoring authority, and London grew dirtier and smokier. In 1886 a week of fog killed between 500 and 700 people, equalling the number of fatalities in the worst cholera years.

When Octavia returned from her travels abroad in 1880, she turned her attention to a new campaigning issue – clean air in our cities and towns. She had been impressed with the *"better out-door life"* that people enjoyed in other European countries and she was convinced that this was not due to better weather but to public gardens and cleaner air. She promised that, on her return, she would see if the Kyrle Society could do something to *"get rid of the smoke"*. Her proposal to set up a sub-committee of the Society to deal with smoke abatement was accepted and it started work in co-operation with the National Health Society.

Octavia stressed the scientific and economic arguments for tackling air pollution:

> The savings ought to be enormous, as the smoke all consists of unconsumed fuel. Some scientific men say that as much as three million out of five million tons annually used in London flies away in smoke and so does harm and no good. .... the mere waste in fuel is considerable, to say nothing of the cost

of extra washing (and) the extra artificial light needed in the day-time.

She was also conversant with the practical measures that could be taken to ameliorate smoke pollution. In her letter to fellow workers in 1881 she states:

66 99 *Every improved grate is both cheaper and better, mainly because it ensures more complete combustion and consequently emits less smoke.*

In November 1881 the National Health Society and the Kyrle Society organised the Smoke Abatement Exhibition in South Kensington. It ran for eleven weeks and was attended by 116,000 people, including engineers, builders and architects. There were displays of smokeless coal-fired grates, stoves and ranges, gas appliances for cooking and heating and different types of coal, including smokeless anthracite. As a result of the exhibition, George Shaw Lefevre, First Commissioner of Works, ordered samples of the best devices to be installed in government buildings. The Duke of Westminster, president of the organising committee and a large property owner in London, instructed his agent to consult with his tenants on the Grosvenor Estate about the use of smokeless stoves.

After the success of the exhibition, Octavia stood back from this campaign as the National Smoke Abatement Society and later the Coal Smoke Abatement Society carried forward the work. Her aim of clean air in London was a long time coming. *"I cannot help thinking that the effort to abate smoke will steadily grow, bringing with it gradual success"*, she wrote, as long ago as 1881. The Clean Air Act was finally passed in 1956 following the great London smog of 1952, which was blamed for 4,000 deaths. There have been no smogs in London since 1962 and by 1971 the reception of winter sunshine had increased by fifty percent since the introduction of the legislation.

2012 - RED CROSS GARDENS IS STILL BEING
USED AS OCTAVIA HILL INTENDED.

OCTAVIA AND EMPLOYMENT

O ctavia regarded her housing management work as much more than putting a roof over people's heads. By assisting her tenants to find work and obtain skills, she believed that they would be self-sufficient and not dependent on charity. She contended that indiscriminate charitable handouts were corrosive and created a *"learned helplessness"* in the recipients. Octavia would have agreed with the aim of the homelessness charity the Big Issue - *"a hand up rather than a handout"*.

Her first experience of providing employment and skills training came when she was only fourteen and manager of the toy-makers at the Ladies' Guild. Here she managed a group of over twenty girls and was involved in toy design, processing orders and marketing goods. She also learnt to keep the books and prepare financial statements – skills she would use in future ventures. It was her apprenticeship in business methods.

In nineteenth century London, employment for the unskilled and labouring classes was erratic and poorly paid. In response, Octavia started the Walmer Street Industrial Experiment in 1870 to provide work and skills training for the people living in the 200 dwellings in the neighbourhood of Walmer Street, Walmer Place and Virgil Place in Marylebone. She wrote up the experiment in two annual reports for the local parish of St Mary's in Bryanston Square.

The project was financed through private donations, and accounts and reports were circulated to all doners to tell them how their contributions had been spent. Sometimes, Octavia used this money to employ tenants to work as painters, bricklayers or window cleaners on the buildings she managed. But through her social contacts she also found work for men and women with a range of employers. Most of the employment she helped provide was short-term to support a family through a difficult time. It was also varied - according to the annual report of 1871 someone was paid 2/6d for playing the violin. This might have been at one of the numerous entertainment events she organised for her tenants.

She created a workroom on site where women did needle work and knitting. In fact the largest item of income in the accounts came from the sale of needlework, which would have included making clothes - in 1871 clothes to the value of £30 were sent to New Zealand. Some of the project funds were used to provide loans so that men and women could buy trade tools to enable them to become self-employed.

The beneficiaries of the Walmer Street Industrial Experiment were systematically processed in a case-work style. A room was provided in Walmer Street which was staffed for half an hour daily to receive applications. Particulars were taken of the needs and skills of every family member. Out of the 200 households she received 133 applications, of which ninety were offered work and forty three were given loans. She made permanent and adequate provision to old people who were past the age of work – *"I have tried to give them small weekly pensions"*. She recognised that working people could seldom save for their old age.

Octavia continued to help her tenants find employment even when the Walmer Street Industrial Experiment closed down. She believed that her scheme of enabling people to work had three advantages: it prevented them from becoming paupers; it gave them self-respect and a sense of responsibility; and it was distinctly educational. She had great faith in the ability of people to better themselves and refused to divide them into the *"deserving"* and *"undeserving"* poor, a popular nineteenth century concept. Octavia wrote in 1871 -

> 66 99 *I have never been able in my own mind to divide those whom I tried to help into two classes of the deserving and undeserving. I have always found that there was bad in the best and good in the worst....this plan enables one to recognise and aid every effort towards better things made by the so-called undeserving.*

In the various tenement blocks she managed she also encouraged the tenants to save through savings clubs. When her women volunteer workers came round to collect the rent they also collected any savings deposits that the families could managed to put to one side. These savings would help the families get through lean times.

VOLUNTEERING
AND FUNDRAISING

ne of the reasons that Octavia was able to put her ideas into practice and to accomplish so much in her life was because she was able to mobilise the resources and skills of her friends, relatives and contacts. Her social networks were extensive and included aristocrats, politicians, the clergy, artists, and social reformers – celebrities who might be characterised as the chattering classes of the nineteenth century. From the ranks of these people she recruited volunteers and persuaded others to donate money to her various projects. She also encouraged those with houses and large gardens in the country to host parties for her tenants on summer day trips out of London.

She managed to maintain the good will and interest of so many people by keeping them informed of her activities and plans through personal letters and detailed accounts of how she spent donations. Like most Victorian women of her class she was a prolific letter writer, but as her work expanded and diversified she found it difficult to cope with the level of personal correspondence. As a result, in 1872 she started to produce annual newsletters of her social enterprises that were sent to all her fellow workers, donors and well-wishers in Britain and overseas. The letters, entitled *Letters to Fellow Workers* were produced between 1872 and 1911 (with the exception of 1884) and around 500 copies were printed each year. These letters helped individual volunteers to see how their efforts were contributing to Octavia's overall programme and how she valued their work. In many of her letters she singled out individuals for praise and gratitude.

As her reputation grew as someone who could be trusted to spend money well on the welfare of the poor, people started to give her funds to administer on their behalf. This money went into the donation account and a report of income and expenditure was published yearly along with the *Letter to Fellow Workers*. Octavia used the money in this account at her own discretion and spent it on a wide range of things over the years. These included open spaces, trees and planting, pensions, training and employment, hospital fees, excursions for tenants, apprenticeships, and emigration. Although she criticised indiscriminate almsgiving, many individual gifts were provided from this fund to help people who had hit hard times due to illness or unemployment.

Separate accounts were kept for the Red Cross Gardens and Hall, the Walmer Street Industrial Experiment and individual properties where people had invested money. Contributions to Octavia's donation account between 1872 and 1911 amounted to over £11,900, which represents well over a £1 million in today's money. The total number of donors to this fund was 787, many of whom contributed frequently over the years. She launched separate appeals for specific projects such as property for the National Trust.

GABLE COTTAGES - DEVELOPED IN 1889

YOUTH WORK AND THE CADET CORPS

hroughout her life Octavia had a deep concern for the education and recreational pursuits of young people. With the opening, in 1888, of the Red Cross Hall in Southwark – *"the parish drawing room"* as she referred to it – Octavia gained the use of a building where she could develop youth activities. Here she encouraged the formation of a girls' club and a boys' club. These clubs met weekly and members had access to microscopes, gymnasium equipment and donated books. Volunteer helpers also organised drama, singing classes and magic lantern shows.

Her most lasting legacy to youth work was her involvement with the Cadet Corps. Despite the pacifist declarations of her mother and friends (including Beatrice and Sidney Webb), she started to organise a Cadet Corps in Southwark for boys under 18 years of age. She countered her mother's objections to the militaristic nature of the scheme by denying that the organisation would *"strengthen a love of war"*. She saw it more as a means of providing working-class boys with *"exercise, discipline, obedience and esprit-de-corps"*. According to her biographer, Moberly Bell,

> Octavia regarded the corps simply as an instrument of education; in her mind its value lay in what it could do for the lads, not in what they corporately could do in the army.

However some of the boys did join the army and went off to fight and die in the Boer War. These young men's lives, along with those of their officers, are commemorated by a plaque in Southwark Cathedral.

She started the cadets in Southwark after seeing the impact such a corps had had on boys in Whitechapel. *"I heard that there was nothing which would gather in some of the most difficult rough boys and do them so much good".* As always, her planning was meticulous. She approached the War Office for assistance and started fund raising for uniforms and a sergeant's pay. She estimated that she would need £100 to start.

The Southwark Cadet Corps was inaugurated on 30th May 1889 by Lord Wolseley[3], the foremost general of his time and a popular military figure. By this time 160 boys had joined, sixty of whom were in uniforms after completing the requisite number of drills. At the end of 1889 Octavia started fund raising for musical instruments and employing a band-master: she felt no Cadet Corps was complete without a band.

By 1890 the ranks of the corps had increased to 398 boys. Demand was so great that the admission of new candidates was suspended until funds were found for more uniforms. When Vauxhall Gardens in South London were opened to the public by the Prince and Princess of Wales in 1890, the Southwark Cadet Corps provided the guard of honour.

Activities were not confined to the environs of Red Cross Hall and Gardens. In July 1890, 110 boys were taken for a week's camping at Churn in Berkshire. This was twenty years before Baden Powell popularised camping with the Boy Scout movement. For many of the boys this outdoor adventure in Berkshire would have been their first experience of life outside the congested streets of London.

In 1890 the War Office recognised the Southwark Corps as the first cadet battalion in London. The national cadet movement developed out of this battalion and by 1909 more than 8,000 boys had passed through the Southwark Cadet Corps. Today the organisation survives as the Army Cadet Force, which puts great emphasis on the development of the cadet as a person and as a good citizen. The force is also involved with the Duke of Edinburgh's Award Scheme.

---

3   Lord Wolseley, was Commander in Chief of the British Army 1895-1901. He saw service in many parts of the then British Empire and was instrumental in modernising the army.

CONCLUDING COMMENTS: OCTAVIA HILL'S MARK ON THE WORLD

Octavia was willing to participate in existing organisations and was the founder of others like the National Trust. However, she had neither a secretary nor treasurer and she didn't bother with annual general meetings or minutes. Records and financial accounts of her work were circulated in her *Letters to Fellow Workers*. She was against unnecessary bureaucracy but was nevertheless very systematic in putting her values into practice and carrying out her own work. Although against a welfare state she tried to promote a type of welfare society where people of all classes recognised their responsibilities towards each other.

She penetrated into some of the worst slums of London and by befriending the tenants gained an understanding of poverty and how it affected family life. She never saw poverty as an abstract concept, illuminated by statistics. To her, poverty was the state in which her tenants, many of whom she knew as friends, struggled to live. She campaigned on issues that would bring about practical change but was reluctant to become involved in theoretical politics and utopian solutions. She neither condemned nor idealised the labouring classes, but saw them as individuals, who, given the right opportunities and encouragement could improve their circumstances by their own efforts. All facets of her work seemed to fit together like a huge jig-saw – believing that humankind does not live by bread alone she was keen to nourish other aspects of her tenants' lives through art, music, culture, sport and a love of the natural world.

To her, work was the main route out of poverty. Unlike many of her contemporaries she was not in favour of state pensions or welfare benefits and was sceptical about indiscriminate almsgiving. Nevertheless, she provided pensions for some of her elderly and infirm tenants with no families, through her donation account. Pragmatism and common sense were at the root of all her actions.

Octavia's influence on British cities was considerable in the years immediately following her death in 1912. In her wake followed a new generation of town planners, case workers, policy makers and social reformers. These included:

Emma Cons, who collaborated with Octavia for many years, starting at Paradise Place. She helped in the development of the Old Vic and the National Theatre, and her niece help found the modern Sadlers Wells theatre.

Canon and Henrietta Barnett founded Toynbee Hall, a multi-purpose community centre, still functioning today in the east end of London. The Barnetts also went on to found Hampstead Garden Suburb, a model of housing development in north London.

Patrick Geddes, the founder of modern town planning, who was introduced to Octavia early on in his career.

Hundreds of women, who became housing managers and members of the Association of Women House Property Managers, which was founded in 1916.

In the second half of the twentieth century, Octavia Hill's views and practices were overshadowed by efforts to provide large numbers of publicly-owned and subsidised dwellings to solve the *"housing problem"*. Thousands of houses had been destroyed in the Second World War and many more, so called *"unfit"* dwellings, were demolished as a result of large-scale municipal redevelopment schemes. Earlier in the century, Octavia had warned that large estates would be difficult to manage because they ignored human scale and the need for defensible space. She also warned that municipal control would be inclined to create inefficient and bureaucratic management, insensitive to tenants' needs. In similar vein, she prophesied that subsidised housing would perpetuate rather than eliminate divisions in society.

What would Octavia be saying and doing today? Judging by her actions she would be out on the estates, listening to tenants and encouraging practical self-help solutions. She would have engaged with community cohesion as an issue and seen the value of mixed communities. She would, you can almost be sure, still be making a big impact.

66 99 *It is a life rather of growth than of change, of development rather than crisis, built up on foundations laid and tested in the now far away past.* Octavia Hill 1900

SARSDEN BUILDINGS WAS MANAGED
BY OCTAVIA HILL FROM 1869

BIBLIOGRAPHY AND FURTHER READING

The following were used as resource material for this publication:

BELL, MOBERLEY,
Octavia Hill, London 1942

BEST, RICHARD,
Octavia Hill and Housing To-day, The Octavia Hill Society Inaugural Lecture 1993

CLAYTON, PETER,
Octavia Hill 1838 – 1912, Wisbech Society and Preservation, 1993

DARLEY, GILLIAN,
Octavia Hill, A Life, Constable, London 1990

HILL, OCTAVIA,
Employment or Alms, London 1871

HILL, OCTAVIA,
Homes of the London Poor. A series of essays, 1870

LOWE, STUART, AND HUGH, DAVID, EDITORS OF
A New Century of Social Housing, Leicester University Press, 1991

WALKER, STEPHEN P,
Octavia Hill and the Experience of Quiet Power and Sympathy, in Accounting and Financial History, July 2006

WHELAN, ROBERT, EDITOR OF
Octavia Hill's Letters to Fellow-Workers 1872-1911, Kyrle Books, London 2005

CHRONOLOGY
OF EVENTS

Political and social events in Octavia's life

	POLITICAL & SOCIAL EVENTS		EVENTS IN OCTAVIA'S LIFE
1837	Victoria becomes Queen.		
		1838	Octavia born in Wisbech.
1839	Parliament rejects first Chartist petition.		
1840	Queen Victoria marries Albert of Saxe-Coburg Gotha.		James Hill declared bankrupt.
1842	Parliament rejects second Chartist petiton		
1843	Modern Painters by John Ruskin published.		
1845	Irish Famine begins		
1846	Repeal of the Corn Laws.		Octavia lives in Finchley London.
1847	Ten Hour Factory Act		
1848	The Communist Manifesto by Karl Marx and Fredrick Engels published Chartist demonstration on Kennington Common.		
1851	Great Exhibition in Hyde Park		
		1852	Octavia moves to Russell Place.
		1853	John Ruskin meets Octavia.
			Continues overleaf...

Year	Historical Events	Year	Octavia Hill's Life
1854–1856	Crimean War fought against Russia.	1855	Octavia starts to train as copyist of painting with John Ruskin.
		1856	Octavia starts working at the Working Men's College.
1857	War with China.		
1859	On the Origin of Species by Charles Darwin published. On Liberty by John Stuart Mill published.		The Hills move to Francis Street and then to Milton Street.
		1860	The Hills move to Nottingham, Place, Marylebone, London.
1861	Death of Prince Albert. Great Expectations by Charles Dickens published.		
1862	International Exhibition South Kensington.		Octavia and Emily open school for girls in Nottingham Place, Marylebone, London.
1863	The Water Babies by Charles Kingsley published.		
1864	First underground railway opened in London.		Octavia begins teaching at Working Women's College.
		1865	Ruskin buys houses in Paradise Place. Octavia's sister Gertrude marries Charles Lewis, stepson of George Eliot (Marion Evans).
1866	The Atlantic telegraph cable is laid.		Ruskin buys houses in Freshwater Place.
1868	Second Reform Act. Trades Unions Congress formed.		
1869	Suez Canal opened.		Octavia joins Marylebone district committee of Charity Organisation Society. She starts managing Barretts Court.
		1870	Octavia starts the Walmer Street Industrial Experiment.

Year	Event		Octavia
1871	Bank Holidays introduced. Middlemarch by George Eliot published.		
		1872	James Hill, Octavia's father, dies and Octavia starts her first Letters to Fellow Workers.
		1875	1875 Octavia's Homes of the London Poor published.
1876	Queen Victoria declared Empress of India. Alexander Graham Bell patents the telephone in the USA.		Princess Alice, Queen Victoria's daughter, visits Octavia's properties.
1877	Society for the Protection of Ancient Buildings founded.		Our Common Land by Octavia published. She becomes engaged to Edward Bond. Ruskin attacks her publicly in Fors Clavigera. Octavia suffers nervous breakdown.
1878	Electric street lighting introduced in London.		
1879	First London telephone exchange opens		
1881	William Morris establishes his Merton Abbey works.		Smoke Abatement Exhibition opens in South Kensington. Octavia gives evidence to the Royal Commission on Housing. She starts managing property for the Ecclesiastical Commissioners.
1882	Electric trams begin in London		
1883	Bitter Cry of Outcast London by Andrew Mearns published.		
1884	Third Reform Act. Art Workers' Guild founded.		Harriot Yorke pays for Crockham Hill in Kent to be built as a country retreat.
			Continues overleaf...

Year		Year	
1885	Karl Benz develops first petrol engine motor vehicle. The Mikado by W S Gilbert and A Sullivan staged.		
		1886	Work starts on Red Cross Cottages and Gardens. The Horace Street Trust is formed.
1887	Queen Victoria's Golden Jubilee Arts and Craft Exhibition Society founded.		Octavia is invited to the Queen's Golden Jubilee.
		1888	Red Cross Hall and Gardens opened by the Archbishop of Canterbury.
		1889	Octavia joins the Committee of the Women's University Settlement in Southwark.
		1890	Vauxhall Park opened.
1891	News from Nowhere by William Morris published. Tess of the D'Urbervilles by Thomas Hardy published.		Octavia moves to 190 Marylebone Road. She forms Kent and Surry committee of the Commons Preservation Society. She contributes to Charles Booth's survey Life and Labour of the people of London.
		1893	Hilly Fields saved. Training courses for social work introduced at the Women's Settlement. Octavia gives evidence to the Royal Commission for Aged Poor.
1895	Trial of Oscar Wilde.		Dinas Oleu at Barmouth becomes first National Trust property.
1897	Queen Victoria's Diamond Jubilee.		
		1898	Octavia's portrait painted by John Singer Sargent.

1899-1902	South African Boer War.	1899	Octavia's involvement with housing in Notting Hill begins. Ruskin dies. (1900)
1901	Death of Queen Victoria and succession of her son Edward VII.		
		1902	Octavia's mother dies.
1903	Emmeline Pankhurst founds the Women's Social and Political Union.		Octavia starts to manage her biggest estate for EC in Walworth South London.
1904	Peaceful picketing during strikes legalised.		
1905	The Automobile Association founded.		
1906	Liberal landside election win.		
1909	Pensions introduced for men and women over 70.		
1910	Florence Nightingale dies.		Miranda Hill dies.
1911	King George succeeds to the throne. Lloyd George's National Insurance Bill for unemployment and sickness insurance is passed.		Octavia writes her last Letter to Fellow-Workers.
1912	Scott reaches the South Pole. The Titanic sinks.		Octavia dies in August in Marylebone.

OPEN SPACES IN OR NEAR LONDON THAT OCTAVIA HILL AND THE KYRLE SOCIETY HELPED SECURE FOR PUBLIC USE

LOCATION	DATE	COMMENTS
Burnham Beeches	1879	The Corporation of London was persuaded to acquire this 540 acre woodland in Buckinghamshire.
Churchyard Bottom Wood	1898	Now known as Queen's Wood in Highgate North London. Offered on favourable terms by Ecclesiastical Commissioners at a cost of £30,000.
Hainault Forest	1906	Octavia supported the efforts of Mr E North Buxton of the Commons' Preservation Society to secure these woodlands near Romford Kent.
Hilly Fields	1892	Purchased for £42,000 by the London County Council with donations mobilized by the Kyrle Society. Located in Lewisham South London.
Horsemonger Lane Gaol	1884	Now known as Newington Gardens, is in Southwark, South London. Kyrle Society campaigned with others to secure this open space. It was opened by Mrs Gladstone, the prime minister's wife in 1884.
Lincoln's Inn Fields	1895	After six years of campaigning the Kyrle Society persuaded the Trustees of Lincoln's Inn Fields in central London - to grant access to the public.

Parliament Hill Fields	1889	Octavia and others raised £52,500 to help secure Parliament Hill Fields, which was purchased by London County Council.
Poors'Land Bethnal Green	1895	Was also known locally as Barmy Park; this garden is now part of a conservation area near Bethnal Green Town Hall, East London.
Postman's Park	1898	A small open space which combines three churchyards, situated between Aldersgate and Little Britain in the City of London. The Kryle Society contributed to the funding.
Purley Beeches	1907	This land was purchased by Croydon local authority after some opposition from ratepayers.
St Anne's Church Yard	1892	Situated in Soho, Central London, this churchyard still provides an open space in the heart of the West End of London.
St George's Gardens	1884	This old burial ground is located off Handel Street in Bloomsbury, London. It was managed by the Kyrle Society until 1884 and is now owned by Camden Council.
St John's Waterloo	1887	This small garden adjacent to the Church is very close to the Octavia Hill Estate properties near Waterloo Station. The church and grounds were bombed during WWII but were rebuilt for the Festival of Britain.
St Peter's Bethnal Green	1884	This quarter of an acre church-yard near Bethnal Green, was originally planted with shrubs and flowers by the Kyrle Society.
		Continues overleaf...

Telegraph Hill Park	1895	With support from the Kryle Society this land in Lewisham South London was purchased from the Haberdashers' Company with a donation from Sir George Livesey. In 2003 the park was restored with a lottery grant.
Vauxhall Park	1890	This South London park was opened by the Prince and Princess of Wales in 1890.
Wandle Trail	1911	This trail, in Carshalton, Surrey, is a nature reserve which runs for eleven miles beside the river Wandle. The Kyrle Society helped to secure some of this land, thereby realising Octavia's vision of putting together a "river path". Part is now owned by the National Trust.
West Wickham Common	1891	Purchased through public contributions. Located on the N.W. Kent and London borders.